INj

7/06

Nice Wheels

Written by Gwendolyn Hooks
Illustrated by Renee Andriani

My First READER

children's press®

A Division of Scholastic Inc.
New York Toronto London Auckland Sydney
Mexico City New Delhi Hong Kong
Danbury, Connecticut

Library of Congress Cataloging-in-Publication Data

Hooks, Gwendolyn.
  Nice wheels / written by Gwendolyn Hooks ; illustrated by Renee Andriani.
      p. cm. — (My first reader)
  Summary: The classmates of a new boy at school find that, although he is in a wheelchair, he can do what they do.
  ISBN 0-516-25179-1 (lib. bdg.)   0-516-25277-1 (pbk.)
  [1. People with disabilities—Fiction. 2. Schools—Fiction.] I. Andriani, Renee, ill. II. Title. III. Series.
  PZ7.H6635Ni 2005
  [E]—dc22
                              2004015300

1 2 3 4 5 6 7 8 9 10 R 14 13 12 11 10 09 08 07 06 05

Note to Parents and Teachers

Once a reader can recognize and identify the 37 words used to tell this story, he or she will be able to successfully read the entire book. These 37 words are repeated throughout the story, so that young readers will be able to recognize the words easily and understand their meaning.

The 37 words used in this book are:

a	friend	made	sure
art	go	music	there
book	he	my	to
boy	I	new	too
can	I'm	not	we
class	in	paints	what
did	is	read	wheelchair
do	know	shares	
don't	laughs	sings	
eat	lunch	sits	

There is a new boy in my class.

He sits in a wheelchair.

Can he do what we do?

I'm not sure. I don't know.

We go to music class.

He sings, too.

We go to art class.

He paints, too.

We read a book.

He laughs, too.

We eat lunch.

He shares, too.

He made a new friend.

I did, too.

ABOUT THE AUTHOR

Gwendolyn Hooks is the author of four books for children. She loves to write, read, swim, and camp outdoors. Hooks lives in Oklahoma City, Oklahoma, with her husband, children, and the family cat, Kitty Kat Hooks.

ABOUT THE ILLUSTRATOR

Renee Andriani, a graduate of Rhode Island School of Design, grew up in Connecticut. Today, she lives in Leawood, Kansas, with her husband, three children, and two dogs. In addition to illustrating children's books, Renee designs and writes greeting cards for Hallmark Cards.